My Favorite Sewing Quotes

In Seattle you haven't had enough coffee until you can thread a sewing machine while it's running. ~Jeff Bezos,

BASIC SEWING BUSINESS FOR BEGINNERS: HOW TO SEW BASICS, LEARN HOW TO SEW CLOTING WITH SEWING MACHINES & FUN PROJECTS FOR MONEY BEGINNER'S CRAFTS GUIDE SERIES

Introduction

The goal of this book is to show you the top 9 sewing ways that you could apply today as a beginner.

This book is going to guide you through the 9 best ways to get started with your first sewing project. This sewing system is going to help achieve this goal. Once you have been able to apply this system, you are automatically going to feel inspired , encouraged, and motivated about your first creative sewing experience and you are most likely going to be hooked for life.

You will be able to identify all the possibilities and creative ways that you can apply as a sewing crafter, and this guide will act as a starting point from where you can explore your exciting sewing path. Maybe you just like to learn some sewing techniques to save some money as a homemaker. There are other individuals who have developed a whole career and passion out of their sewing skills. In my book series called "From Passion To Profit", I have talked to countless crafters who have developed their business around sewing and made a fortune with it.

Sewing is fun and profitable. This book is there to get you inspired and mentally stimulated about the wonderful world of sewing. Hopefully, this book is inspirational to you, and hopefully it turns you into a very passionate sewer who is going to be able to turn passion into more than just a hobby.

You can use this guide as a starting point from where you have all the options to develop your passion for sewing into a sustainable business or a hobby that you like to do on a weekend.

You can use the guide in a very creative way and it is up to you to pick your favorite sewing ways and then go your path from there.

I suggest that you first go through the whole guide and once you have familiarized yourself with the top 9 ways of sewing for a beginner, you can go and explore more cool sewing stuff via the "Resources" chapters and the "Interactive Ways For More Cool Sewing Nuggets" chapter.

Once you are done with your exploration, proceed to the chapter "The Next Step" from where I am going to guide you to what to do next and how to continue with your sewing path.

Getting started with a sewing project on your own and without knowing what to do first in order to be successful with your first sewing project can be a very frustrating task if you do not know how to go about it.

The good news is that you can use this guide and learn everything that you need to know about sewing in order to make this a fun and exciting experience for you. You can do this over one weekend and once you get the whole idea of what is involved in order to make a sewing project a successful one, you can go from there and look into more advanced and professional type of sewing projects.

By going through this guide and by picking the ways that might apply best to your own situation, you are going to become an expert in sewing over a weekend's time!

The guide includes 9 simple, easy, quick, and applicable sewing ways that you can apply today in order to get started with your first sewing project.

To achieve this goal, you must start going through the whole guide first. Once you are done pick your favorite ways and apply them without delay.

You are in no way limited to these 9 ways because there are many more ways available to start your sewing project.

The goal here is to provide you with the easiest, most usable, and most basic to consume information that you are going to need for your first sewing project.

This is why I decided to stick to the top 9 ways that are not going to overwhelm you. I feel that information overload is doing you harm because a cluttered mind is a mind that does not take action.

The goal is simply to get a general overview of the top ways and to get you encouraged and started. Once you have a starting point, you can quickly move to the next step. This way you will get a basic overview without getting stuck and you are able to quickly move forward with your first sewing project. You can quickly switch between mental work, research, and learning more cool nuggets about sewing and the actual sewing practice.

Once you have gone through the 9 ways of sewing, you can proceed to the Resources Section and the Interactive Ways Of More Cool Sewing Nuggets Sections to learn even more cool stuff about sewing and to continue your learning path.

After having mastered the basics and having developed a passion for sewing, you can move forward in your sewing path and learn about the advanced sewing techniques and projects.

Be aware that I will constantly be updating this book so that it will always reflect the top ways and resources of sewing that a beginner is looking for. Make sure to check for updates regularly. I will inform you about the latest updates on my Facebook page, too.

Lastly, I hope that this book is going to help you get the most out of your first sewing project, and I hope that the guide will get you started the right way so that you are going to be hooked and passionate about sewing like so many others who have been able to start their own lucrative from passion to profit type businesses. I hope you will go the same profitable and passionate way as so many crafters that I have been able to interview and talk to over the years.

Let's get started with the top nine exciting ways of sewing for a beginner...

First Way: Choosing Your Machine

Learning to sew can be very difficult and a tough skill to learn at first, but with the right kind of guidelines it can be turned into a fun and exciting project that you can get started with over the weekend.

Let's talk about some of the considerable ways of sewing for beginners.

First, as a sewing beginner, you will be required to know your way around your sewing machine. Machine sewing techniques are usually the same no matter what type of sewing machine model you are operating. Before you begin to sew, you will be asked to set up your sewing machine. You can get the guidelines on how to set up your sewing machine in the manual that comes together with your sewing machine. Just have a quick browse through the manual and familiarize yourself with the most important operations.

The manual is usually included and you will find it inside the package. If you can not find your manual, go to the website of the brand of your sewing machine model because the producer of the model is required to carry a manual that goes with each sewing machine model.

On the site you can either order another copy of the manual or you will find any other useful information that might be helpful

to you and teach you how to get a copy of the manual that you need for your machine.

For example, there is a very cool sewing manual site from where you can locate your manual that corresponds to your specific sewing machine model and you can search the manuals by brand and model.

Do a search in Google and the other big search engines for the following search string: "sewing machine manuals".

You can find these types of sites as a result from searches like this:

http://www.sewingmachinemanuals.com[1]

http://homeappliance.manualsonline.com/manuals/device/sewing_machine.html

You can also look at Vintage Sewing Machine Manuals or search for "vintage sewing machine manuals or pdfs" on places like eBay. eBay is the biggest repository for these types of vintage sewing manuals.

Let's continue to the second way of sewing that is choosing your sewing techniques.

---

1.   http://www.sewingmachinemanuals.com/

Second Way: Choosing Your Sewing Technique

Beginners usually get started with the basic sewing techniques. These techniques include the hem stitch, the double stitch, and the directional stitch. You can go ahead and get guidelines on how to make these stitches by using a beginner's sewing book that explains all the sewing techniques with pictures and operational guidelines. There are various beginners books which include the "Readers Digest" guide and "Encyclopedic Sewing" guides.

As a beginner, it is always important to start small so that you do not get disappointed. You can get started by mending simple torn clothes and sewing button holes. If you have children use their clothes to get started because kids rip their pants, shirts, and skirts frequently. Getting started your sewing project with your kid's clothing is perfect because if you make a mistake it does not really matter. Kids are always up for some funny looking results and children's clothing is the least expensive to replace.

Stitching requires to learn the specific sewing techniques that are acquired to learn. It takes time to get used to these sewing techniques, but if you are passionate about sewing you will have no trouble with the repetitive sewing exercises.

If you do not get it right the first time, do not get discouraged. You will get it right with enough practice.

If you do not want to learn how to operate a sewing machine, you can stick to sewing by hand. This is mainly applied to sewing of buttons.

Experts are saying that sewing by hand is a great way to learn how to sew and to appreciate the art of sewing. Once you are getting better at sewing by hand you can learn how to operate a sewing machine. It is important to master the basics of sewing by hand first before getting overwhelmed with too advanced sewing techniques that require a machine.

This concludes the first way of sewing and you are now ready to learn about the next way of sewing.

Third Way: The Different Sewing Projects

As a beginner, you absolutely need to understand these basic sewing methods when starting up your first sewing project.

The following three are the basic sewing methods.

Perfect Seam Sewing Project

A seam is as line of stitches that is used for holding two fabrics. In order to get desirable results, the seam linen needs to be evenly and straight. A seam is the most basic concept that a beginner needs to learn as a method of sewing.

The Anatomy of A Dart

Making a dart is another method of sewing that usually refers to, a fold that is sewn for the purpose of providing a three dimensional shape to a certain fabric. A dart is normally required to fit in perfectly to the details of a fabric.

In order to make a perfect fit: one will be required to make various alterations.

The French Seam

A French seam is a technique that is normally used for enclosing a seam allowance on the inside part of a sewn item. This seam is used on people with very sensitive skin as it leaves the edges of the fabric soft.

Let's continue with the many ways of stitches that a beginner should know about.

Fourth Way: The Many Ways Of Stitches

Stitches are the basis of needlecraft. You need it not only for sewing, but also for knitting, crochet and embroidery work. Whether you are working with the needle by hand or by machine, you will need to know about different kinds of stitches.

In this chapter, I will try to underline some of the most important sewing stitches. Let's first talk about some of the basic stitches that you need to know as a beginner.

The Blanket Stitch:

The blanket stitch is used as a decorative stitch on many garments and pieces of clothing. Besides blankets, it is also applied on outerwear, sportswear, sweaters, swimsuits, home decoration items, and home furnishings, etc. There are many styles of producing the blanket stitch.

The term "blanket stitch" has become a verb that describes the application of this stitch.

http://www.youtube.com/watch?v=eXkSE2TTF4s

The Running Stich:

The running stitch is the basic stitch in sewing and also in embroidery. The running stitch is kind of the starting point of all the others more advanced stitches. The running stitch is done by passing the needle in from one way and it comes out the other way.

The running stitch is the way to sew basic seams. Sewing via the running stitch gives you more visibility of the thread on the top layer rather than on the bottom layer.

Check out this video for learning the running stitch:

http://www.youtube.com/watch?v=KUC6kkuYZBw

The Basting Stitch:

This basting stitch is a kind of running stitch that is used to hold two pieces of fabric together. If you want to sew something and you are afraid it will budge from its place (therefore making the sides uneven) you can apply the basting stitch in order to hold two pieces together. The basting stitch looks like a dashed line (- -)

Tip for the Basting Stitch:

When using a basting stitch try using a thread of contrasting colors so that it becomes easier for you to see and remove the thread after finishing the final sewing project.

Check out this video for the basting stitch:

http://www.youtube.com/watch?v=vG4-6LRKwfk

The Backstitch Stitch:

This stitch can either be used to outline shapes or to create a base for some other stitches. The backstitch stitch can even help you sew through several layers of material or fabric and you can use it to repair a seam. It is a stitch that is used in embroidery and for sewing projects. The stitches are backwards as the name suggests. The stitches do form lines and this stitch is usually used to outline shapes. It can also be used to add more elaboration to embroidery. This stitch is perfect for making fine details and lines.

http://www.youtube.com/watch?v=n04lLVqOEjA

The Overcast Stitch:

The overcast stitch is used on unfinished and raw materials and fabrics. It is mainly used to finish the edges of the materials. It consists of diagonal stitches at the edge of a fabric or material.

You can also use the overcast stich to avoid unravelling. To make the overcast stitch you proceed like this. Go from the inside and loop over the edge of the fabric and then take the needle to the back again. It will look like a ./././ (the dot is the entering point).

http://www.youtube.com/watch?v=q6IFSeCKmzc

The Cross Stitch:

As the name cross stitch suggests it, it is a stitch in the form of an X or a +.

It is a very useful sewing stitch because you can combine the X stitches and the + stitches and like this you can make a nice pattern out of it.

http://www.youtube.com/watch?v=OLYdbatulwM

The Buttonhole Stitch:

The buttonhole stitch is used to make buttonholes and this stitch kind of resembles the overcast stitch. Another version of the buttonhole stitch is the blanket stitch.

http://www.youtube.com/watch?v=ME3qZMol4RI

The Whip Stitch:

The whip stitch can be used for seaming two fabrics or materials together. You can either sew the fabrics with the right side or with the wrong side together. It is kind of a overcast stitch, but the whip stitch is tighter and the loops are closer to one another.

http://www.youtube.com/watch?v=v9kGyZDWZcA

Tip for the Whip Stitch:

Leave a tail of your thread and loop several times over it so that the thread does not stand out.

The Blind Hem Stitch:

The blind hem stitch is widely used for hems and if you choose a color that matches closer to the material that you are using it really is an invisible type of stitch and very useful for delicate items.

http://www.youtube.com/watch?v=jdKe9crSHac

The Vertical Hem or Couch Stitch:

This stitch is also known as couch stitch and as the name suggests it is a very useful and durable stitch. Like the blind hem stitch it is almost invisible which makes this stich perfect for a couture stitch. If you are looking for a very neat and unobtrusive finish of your item, I suggest using this stitch.

You can end the seam of your item that you are working on on the inside of the fabric. As the name suggests this kind of stitch is used a lot with the finishing of couches.

You can watch an instructional video of the couch stitch here: http://www.ehow.com/video_4940673_sew-couch-stitch.html

Fivth Way: Sewing Practice Sheets

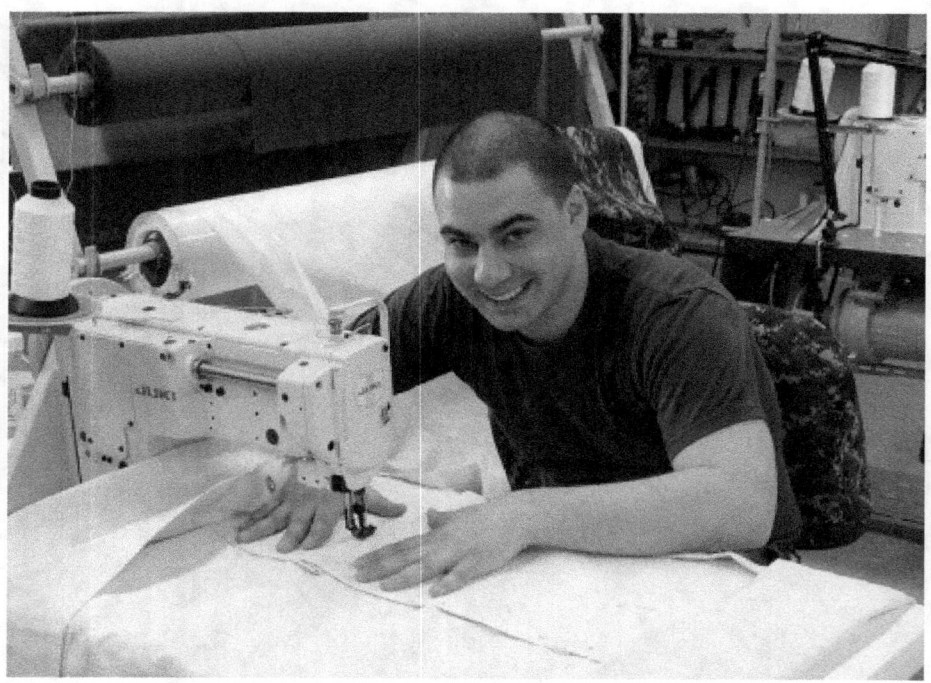

Learning how to sew over the weekend can be a very fun and exciting project for a beginner. However, some who decide to start sewing get frustrated in the very beginning of the process because sewing takes practice and practice requires patience.

This is the reason why most beginners quit and get into another craft that is more forgiving so that even a beginner can have some good results. Sewing on the other hand requires meticulous sewing skills with the needle by hand or machine and if a beginner makes a small mistakes with sewing, the results can be very discouraging.

In order to make your first sewing project a success, start simple. Choose easy patterns and fabrics to work with. Potholders and wrap skirts may not be the most interesting way to spend your time. However, spending time perfecting the basic techniques of sewing will save you a lot of heartache later. Use practice sewing sheets before starting any projects.

You can find them by searching Google for words like: "sewing sheets", "sewing practice sheets for beginners", "sheets for sewing", etc.

Here is a sewing practice sheet for beginners. You can print it out and start your daily practice with these types of practice sheets:

http://www.edonyourown.com/crafts/SewingPracticeSheet.pdf

These will help you practice your techniques that you are working with on that specific day without getting fabric knotted up in your machine. You must be very conscious about the fact that with sewing you do not have the liberty to cut corners when practicing your technique.

Take your time and get it right from the beginning and like this you will develop a passion for it right from the beginning. A solid foundation from the very start will prove valuable when you are ready to move onto more advanced and difficult sewing techniques.

Invite a family member or friend that shares your interest and develop a buddy system so that you can share your first successes. Learning how to sew with others will minimize the frustration and heartache that is very tough specifically in the beginning.

Let's look at some success ingredients that a beginner must absolutely take advantage of.

Sixth Way: Your Magical Success Ingredient

Magical Success Ingredient Number 1

Keeping the pressure on the pedal of your sewing machine at a moderate pace can be tricky. If you go too fast, your sewing machine will zip through the fabric and create crooked, uneven lines on your fabric.

Be sure that your needle is on the down position and ease down slowly on the pedal when you begin with your first sewing project. Make a mental note of the pressure that you are applying and when you get the pressure at a moderate pace, try to replicate the ease of your foot placement on the pedal to this point every time you start with your sewing project.

Magical Success Ingredient Number 2

Keep an iron handy next to your machine and don't skip the iron pressing step of your sewing project that you are working on. Pressing keeps your seams straight and keeps the fabric from bunching up in an awkward way. Press frequently and use a press cloth to prevent burning or scorching.

If you do not have a press cloth, you can use a linen cloth as a suitable substitute. Items that fold over like wallets and similar items will close easier from the pressing. To press, hold the iron down for a few seconds over the area that has just been sewn and apply light pressure.

Do not stretch the fabric as it will ruin the stitches. After 2-3 seconds, lift the iron back up carefully. Repeat the process to remove puckers and to flatten seams, stitches, and corners.

Seventh Way: Cutting Tools That Make It Easy

Let's look at yet another way that you have to keep in mind as a beginner and as you are learning how to sew over the weekend.

Investing in a self-healing mat, a rotary cutter, and a clear ruler will help you cut up your fabric. This makes the lines straighter and allows you to cut through multiple layers of fabric all at once. If you need to cut multiple pieces of fabric that are all the same size, then take your first piece of fabric and make sure you measure it out perfectly.

Place your perfectly cut piece over the other fabric you want to cut and lay your clear ruler on the edge of the measured cut fabric. Cut around this piece of fabric. you should end up with several pieces of fabric perfectly measured at the same size.

Resources:
Easy cutting mats and self-healing mat:
http://www.youtube.com/watch?v=NfzX0QNCdoM
http://www.youtube.com/watch?v=75WYs54col8
Rotary Cutter:
http://www.youtube.com/watch?v=ToKiIYT7mAI
Clear Ruler for Sewing:

http://www.youtube.com/watch?v=2RgWV0ZvrPQ

Eighth Way: Polyester The Way To Go

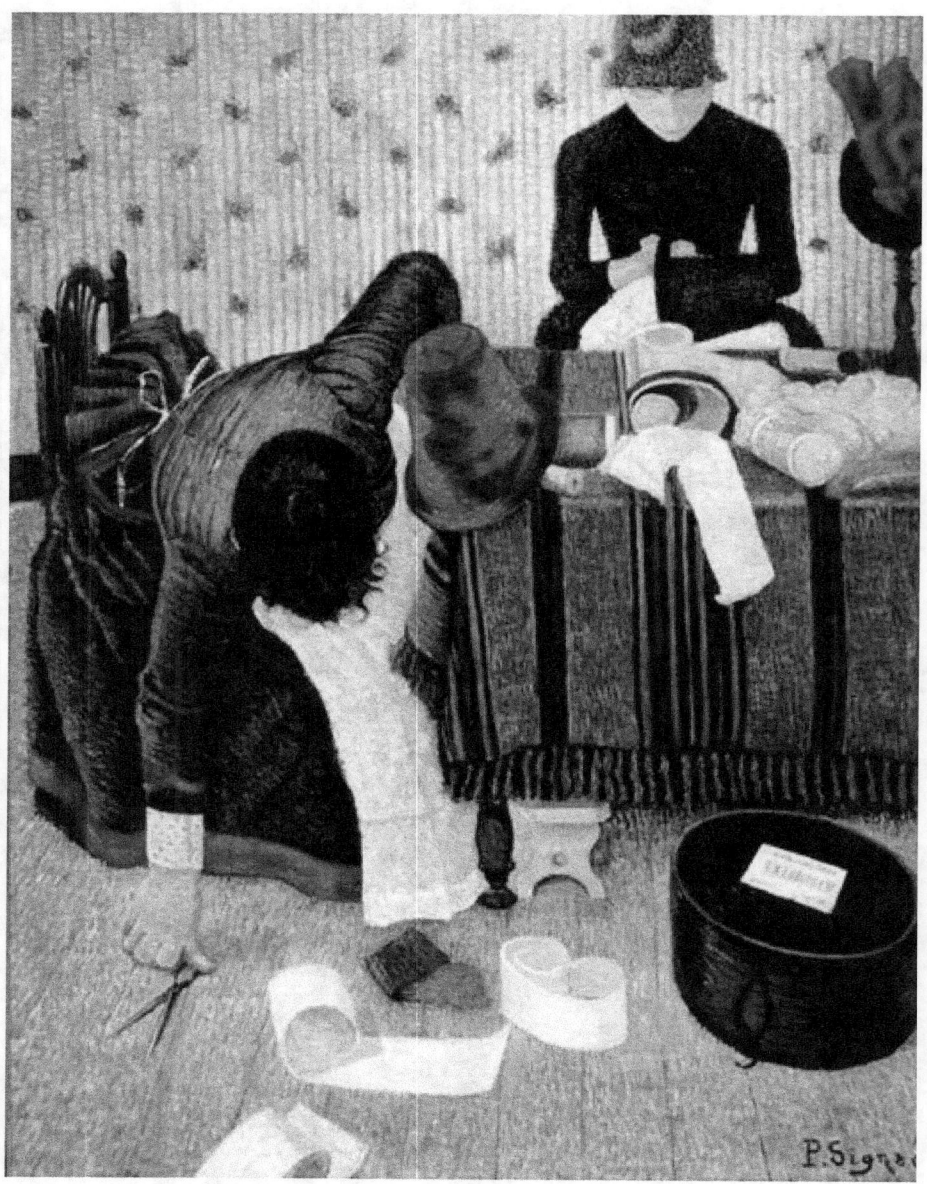

The most important tool that you need for sewing no matter if you sew by hand or by machine is the thread. Let's talk about the polyester thread first because as a beginner you do need to know about the many uses of this type of thread.

Your goal is to exercise as much as possible and you need lots of thread to get started. It is best to use the least expensive option first.

As a beginner, you should be aware of the main characteristics that come with the polyester thread because polyester thread has many advantages.

Let's get started with some historical facts first. Polyester thread was first introduced in the 60's. Before that time, thread was really only made from natural sources. Polyester thread was introduced in a wide variety of vivid colors and the thread was much stronger than what had been available up to that point. The traditional cotton thread is fragile and has the tendency to break.

A beginner might ask the question, but how do you know when polyester thread is the best choice for a sewing project?

To give the best answer, let's break it down and look at the different fibers to see if polyester thread is better to use or not.

Natural Fibers

If you are working with fabrics that are made out of natural fibers, then the best choice for you is to really use a 10% cotton thread. Why? The cotton thread is less likely to pucker at the seams that you are working on and it will fade in color over the lifetime of the garment. Do not be confused and think that cheaper cotton thread is better. The less expensive cotton thread is fabricated from the leftovers of the better quality thread materials. If you buy this variety of thread, you do run the risk of having it splinter and split as you are trying to thread your needle.

Synthetic Fibers

The goal is to match the thread to the type of the materials that you are working with. Polyester thread is the better choice for you when you are working with fabrics that are made from synthetic fibers. If you are using this type of synthetic thread in a sewing machine, be sure to wind it on the bobbin very slowly. The polyester thread has the tendency to stretch if it is pulled and you certainly want to avoid puckering along the seams of the item that you are working on. Once the puckering happens, use an iron to get rid of it.

When working with this this type of thread on your sewing machine, it is well worth the effort to take the time to practice some sewing lines on a scrap piece or piece of fabric before you are going to get started with your sewing project.

Polyester thread in general is the better choice if you are sewing sportswear and outerwear. Cotton thread will rot as time goes on and if it is exposed to the environment. It is possible to purchase a thread that is a blend and that contains cotton and polyester, but this variety does tend to shred in the needle and more so than threads that are made from a single type of fiber only.

Quilting

When choosing a thread for your quilting project, it might be worth considering using a polyester thread that is cotton covered. This way, you get a thread that is extra strong for use in your sewing machine with the softness associated with the quilt's cotton fabric. This thread can also be used by those who prefer to sew their quilted item by hand.

Embroidery

Polyester thread is a popular and economical option for embroidery projects. Polyester thread looks similar to rayon thread and will not shrink, fade, or even bleed. You can buy the thread in a variety of colors, too. The polyester thread is slightly less shiny than a rayon thread, but they certainly can be used in the same embroidery project, if you like. It would be very difficult to tell the difference between the two types of threads.

I hope that you can see by now that using polyester thread for sewing has many advantages and uses. Take some time to consider your sewing project. You will be able to make your choice depending on your sewing project and needs.

Ninth Way: Ways To Get Better

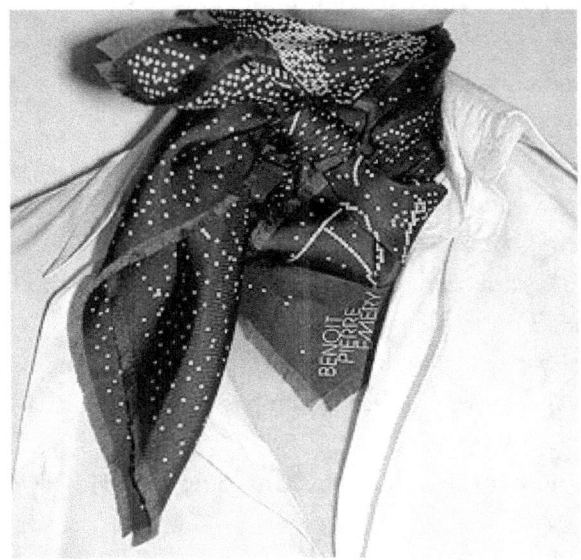

There is absolutely no shortcut or easy way how to learn sewing on the push of a button because sewing is a science and an art at the same time. Sewing requires skills and practice and without repeating the basic sewing exercises over and over again, it will be very difficult for you to advance. If you have the passion for sewing and if you like the physical aspect of the operation, you will become a master at it over time. If not it will be much tougher for you to develop a passion for sewing.

A lot of practice and time is required with sewing. You can only master the numerous techniques of sewing by doing it over and over again and by not getting tired of it.

You can also take advantage of other experts in the sewing field and join a sewing community that helps you stay motivated and focused. A sewing community like:

https://www.threadbias.com/forums
http://sewingforum.com/forum/index.php

Joining a community like these two sewing forums will help you stay encouraged and you will stick to sewing because it is an enjoyable experience. It is fun to participate in an open and live community and to share ideas about the latest sewing techniques, resources, and technologies about sewing. You will find buddies in the sewing community and this will help you become more effectively and advance with your sewing skills, too.

It is in such clubs that you will be able to learn the best techniques and learn about the best fabrics and materials that are available in the marketplace.

If you decide to go into sewing in a professional way, I absolutely recommend joining these two forums today and introduce yourself as the first step because this will hold you accountable for your sewing project.

There is no easy way out on how to perfect your skills in sewing. One simply requires practice and more practice. Sewing is a technique that requires time to master.

You can only master the numerous techniques of sewing by doing it over and over again.

If you do not like to join an active sewing community, you can also find an unlimited amount of online treasures. You will be able to find many sewing technique courses available in electronic format, and you can buy them on places like Amazon, eBay, Udemy, and Etsy. Please look at the resources section below to find more of these sewing marketplaces that you can use to buy educational sewing related products and to sell your finished sewing products, too.

There is not only Etsy that is going to be available to you and you must think beyond marketplaces like Etsy in order to profit from all the opportunities that are available to you.

The resources section will show you all the marketplaces that you can take advantage from. Once you are good at sewing, you can sell your unique product line to marketplaces around the world. Once you are at the point where you can sell your goods, things really are going to become very exciting and fun for you because all your hard work developing your sewing skills is going to pay off in a big way.

I highly suggest to a beginner to stick to your daily exercises and to advance your sewing skills. If you develop a passion for it and if you can relate to the materials that you are working with, you will be able to continue and advance. If you like the touch and feel of the fabrics and the tools, I highly recommend to stick to it and to invest the time and effort to come to a point where you can profit and make money from it.

I have another series about sewing and it is called the "From Passion To Profit" series. In this series I am showing you many sewing success stories and sewing opportunities that sewing experts are tapping into. The sewing experts that are featured in the sewing success stories are revealing the most critical success ingredients that helped them to become a sustainable sewing business. They are revealing some of the most unique sewing opportunities that are available for every passionate sewer to tap into and make money from. They are also revealing their most successful methods, strategies, resources. Best of all they are sharing their blueprints for a successful and lucrative sewing business.

When sewing your first project, it is also advisable that you only choose something you are highly interest in. If you have a liking for skirts and skirt designs then it is highly advisable to sew a skirt because this will make you stick to the end of the project.

Rewarding yourself is also a very important concept to apply and you absolutely must reward yourself in the beginning. Rewarding yourself with a nice drink or some sweets has a very powerful psychological effect on your future behavior and on your mindset.

Take the time to pat yourself on the back and enjoy a nice meal and glass of wine at the end of the day. You can also enjoy a nice cool drink or a piece of chocolate after you have finished your daily sewing chores. Using the psychological concept of rewards will make you stick to your sewing project and will help you restart with a positive mindset the next day.

Sewing buddies and participating in an active sewing forum will help you stick to it, too, because this will hold you accountable and you have to put effort into your work in order to be able to report your results.

In my opinion the psychological concept of rewarding yourself, being passionate for what you are doing, and having a sewing buddy are the three most powerful ways that you can actively apply in order to stick to your sewing project and to quickly advance from a beginner to a sewing expert.

Once you are on the advanced and the expert level, you will be able to tap into the unlimited sewing opportunities that are available to you today.

Next, you can go ahead and learn how to turn your passion into profit and continue your educational path with sewing by applying the concept of the ongoing learning experience.

Conclusion

It is highly advisable that you pick something interesting like a sewing project that you are able to finish. This will encourage and motivate you to stick to the sewing project which in turn helps you advance and get better without overwhelming yourself right in the beginning.

Give yourself a fair chance for success with your first sewing project because otherwise you will become a quitter and never finish a project. Give yourself a trial period and test your qualifications in a very objective manner. This is why I put this information in the form of a guide so that you can go through this guide within a weekend. A weekend gives you plenty of time to decide if this is for you or not.

Going through a guide like this helps you identify if you qualify for sewing and if you do, you should absolutely progress with your sewing path.

If you do not develop a passion for the materials and the sewing techniques, and if you do not like the fact that sewing is something that requires lots of time and practice, I recommend not to force yourself into it because I have talked to many crafters who instead of sewing choose a different path into another craft like jewelry making, or crocheting, or working with hair.

Not everyone is cut out for sewing because it requires meticulous sewing skills and sometimes you are excited about the idea of making your own wardrobe or becoming a fashion designer, but you might recognize while going through the process that it is not exactly what makes you happy.

In this case, it might be best to try out another craft that requires less practice and more creativity on your part. There are many options that are open to you because you probably are already a person who loves working with crafts.

It is a good thing to be able to identify what you do not like and proceed with another opportunity that waits for you. You have a limitless amount of opportunities at your fingertips because crafting is very popular and there are more and more crafting techniques available for you to explore. The more you explore the quicker you will identify which one you want to stick with and develop a passion for.

One of my friends, for example, tried many types of crafting projects for many years without sticking to a particular one. She finally followed another passionate crafter and followed his public domain blueprint. She went from trying out all kinds of crafts to photography. She finally found her passion with photography, and she is now a top seller on Etsy.

Make sure to explore all your options before you lock yourself down to one single technique and then make a business out of your true passion and monetize it.

Let's head over to The Resources section and the Interactive Ways Of More Cool Saving Nuggets section and continue exploring the exciting world of sewing.

To your success with sewing

70+ Sewing Resources

http://www.sewingpatternsonthenet.com/spn_website_003.htm[1]
    http://www.burdastyle.com[2]
    http://subtlepatterns.com[3]
    http://www.patterntap.com[4]
    http://www.spoonflower.com[5]
    http://www.mccall.com/home.html
    http://www.burdastyle.com[6]
    http://sewing.patternreview.com[7]
    http://oliverands.com[8]
    http://www.youcanmakethis.com[9]
    http://www.hotpatterns.com[10]
    http://sewing.org[11]
    http://www.sewingmamas.com[12]
    http://tipnut.com/22-free-pincushion-patterns
    http://www.freeneedle.com[13]
    http://www.allcrafts.net/sewing.htm
    http://wwwearables.com[14]
    http://totallystitchin.net[15]
    http://www.fitzpatterns.com[16]
    http://www.favoritethings.net[17]
    http://www.momspatterns.com[18]

---

1. http://www.sewingpatternsonthenet.com/spn_website_003.htm

2.   http://www.burdastyle.com/

3.   http://subtlepatterns.com/

4.   http://www.patterntap.com/

5.   http://www.spoonflower.com/

6.   http://www.burdastyle.com/

7.   http://sewing.patternreview.com/

8.   http://oliverands.com/

9.   http://www.youcanmakethis.com/

10.   http://www.hotpatterns.com/

11.   http://sewing.org/

12.   http://www.sewingmamas.com/

13.   http://www.freeneedle.com/

14.   http://wwwearables.com/

15.   http://totallystitchin.net/

16.   http://www.fitzpatterns.com/

17.   http://www.favoritethings.net/

http://www.jalie.com[19]
http://www.pursepatterns.com[20]
http://www.threadsmagazine.com[21]
http://www.patternschool.com[22]
http://www.decadesofstyle.com[23]
http://www.folkwear.com[24]
http://babypatterns.atspace.com/overview.html
http://sewing.com[25]
http://underwear.sew-ing.com[26]
http://sensibility.com[27]
http://www.stretchy.org[28]
http://sewfunpatterns.com[29]
http://panty.hanty.net[30]
http://www.lanetzliving.net[31]
http://www.lanetzliving.net[32]
http://vpll.org[33]
http://thedomesticdiva.wordpress.com[34]
http://www.trulyvictorian.com[35]
http://oldpatterns.com[36]
http://www.wildginger.com[37]
http://www.urbanthreads.com[38]

18.   http://www.momspatterns.com/

19.   http://www.jalie.com/

20.   http://www.pursepatterns.com/

21.   http://www.threadsmagazine.com/

22.   http://www.patternschool.com/

23.   http://www.decadesofstyle.com/

24.   http://www.folkwear.com/

25.   http://sewing.com/

26.   http://underwear.sew-ing.com/

27.   http://sensibility.com/

28.   http://www.stretchy.org/

29.   http://sewfunpatterns.com/

30.   http://panty.hanty.net/

31.   http://www.lanetzliving.net/

32.   http://www.lanetzliving.net/

33.   http://vpll.org/

34.   http://thedomesticdiva.wordpress.com/

35.   http://www.trulyvictorian.com/

36.   http://oldpatterns.com/

37.   http://www.wildginger.com/

38.   http://www.urbanthreads.com/

http://www.homesew.com[39]
http://www.pastpatterns.com[40]
http://www.whatthecraft.com/tutorials.php
http://thelongthread.com/?p=669
http://www.e-patternscentral.com[41]
http://www.u-handbag.com[42]
http://www.clothkits.co.uk/index.php
http://www.craftbits.com/project/super-cool-wallet
http://www.freepatterns.com[43]
http://www.patternsoftime.com[44]
http://www.pinkchalkfabrics.com[45]
http://www.denverfabrics.com[46]
http://www.sew4home.com[47]
http://indietutes.blogspot.com[48]
http://www.fatquartershop.com[49]
http://www.ericabunker.com[50]
http://sewingstars.com/mousepattern.htm
http://www.etsy.com[51]
http://www.dawanda.com[52]
http://www.spoonflower.com[53]
http://www.purlbee.com[54]
http://www.craftster.org/bestof2007
http://www.100sewinglinks.com/cgi-bin/ldb/ldb.pl
http://sewing.craftgossip.com[55]
http://www.threadsmagazine.com/item/26229/join-a-sewing-community-online

39.   http://www.homesew.com/

40.   http://www.pastpatterns.com/

41.   http://www.e-patternscentral.com/

42.   http://www.u-handbag.com/

43.   http://www.freepatterns.com/

44.   http://www.patternsoftime.com/

45.   http://www.pinkchalkfabrics.com/

46.   http://www.denverfabrics.com/

47.   http://www.sew4home.com/

48.   http://indietutes.blogspot.com/

49.   http://www.fatquartershop.com/

50.   http://www.ericabunker.com/

51.   http://www.etsy.com/

52.   http://www.dawanda.com/

53.   http://www.spoonflower.com/

54.   http://www.purlbee.com/

55.   http://sewing.craftgossip.com/

http://sew-whats-new.com[56]

http://www.myhappysewingplace.com/2013/02/sew-grateful-week-why-i-love-sewing.html

http://www.sewingmachinemanuals.com[57]

http://homeappliance.manualsonline.com/manuals/device/sewing_machine.html

http://www.edonyourown.com/crafts/SewingPracticeSheet.pdf

http://www.sewingmachinemanuals.com[58]

http://www.edonyourown.com/crafts/SewingPracticeSheet.pdf

https://www.threadbias.com/forums

http://sewingforum.com/forum/index.php

56.   http://sew-whats-new.com/

57.   http://www.sewingmachinemanuals.com/

58.   http://www.sewingmachinemanuals.com/

250+ Creative & Inspirational Craft Resources

Sewing Craft Ideas & Inspiration For Creative Research & Product Creation + Top Sewing Marketplaces Online

http://www.dawanda.com[1]

Udemy.com[2]

http://www.etsy.com[3]

http://www.pinterest.com[4]

https://www.udemy.com/courses/search?q=sewing

http://www.dawanda.com[5]

http://www.etsy.com[6]

http://www.pinterest.com[7]

http://www.fiverr.com[8]

http://www.wallhogs.com[9]

http://www.redbubble.com/shop/top+selling+iphone-cases

http://www.deviantart.com[10]

http://www.zazzle.com[11]

---

1. http://www.dawanda.com/

2.   http://answerszone.info/fast-udemy-cash/

3.   http://www.etsy.com/

4.   http://www.pinterest.com/

5.   http://www.dawanda.com/

6.   http://www.etsy.com/

7.   http://www.pinterest.com/

8.   http://www.fiverr.com/

9.   http://www.wallhogs.com/

10.   http://www.deviantart.com/

11.   http://www.zazzle.com/

http://www.artfire.com[12]
http://www.cafepress.com[13]
http://www.ebay.com[14]
http://www.art.com[15]
http://www.allposters.com[16]
http://www.shortrunposters.com[17]
http://www.wallhogs[18]
http://www.kickstarter.com[19]
http://www.spoonflower.com/welcome
http://store.vervante.com/c/v/bookstore.html?login_c=book-store
https://www.printfection.com/account/register.php
http://www.spreadshirt.com[20]
http://www.customink.com[21]
http://blurb.com[22]
http://www.myownlabels.com[23]
http://www.printpelican.com[24]

12.   http://www.artfire.com/

13.   http://www.cafepress.com/

14.   http://www.ebay.com/

15.   http://www.art.com/

16.   http://www.allposters.com/

17.   http://www.shortrunposters.com/

18.   http://www.wallhogs/

19.   http://www.kickstarter.com/

20.   http://www.spreadshirt.com/

21.   http://www.customink.com/

22.   http://blurb.com/

23.   http://www.myownlabels.com/

24.   http://www.printpelican.com/

http://www.shortrunposters.com[25]

http://www.artfire.com[26]

http://www.mpix.com[27]

http://www.snapfish.com/snapfish/welcome

http://acidflyers.com[28]

http://www.visionbedding.com[29]

http://www.venuspuzzle.com[30]

http://www.getetched.com[31]

http://www.bagettes.com[32]

http://www.printfection.com[33]

http://www.udemy.com[34]

http://www.printpelican.com[35]

http://www.treasureknit.com[36]

http://www.visionbedding.com[37]

http://www.ontapestry.com[38]

http://www.getetched.com[39]

---

25.   http://www.shortrunposters.com/

26.   http://www.artfire.com/

27.   http://www.mpix.com/

28.   http://acidflyers.com/

29.   http://www.visionbedding.com/

30.   http://www.venuspuzzle.com/

31.   http://www.getetched.com/

32.   http://www.bagettes.com/

33.   http://www.printfection.com/

34.   http://www.udemy.com/

35.   http://www.printpelican.com/

36.   http://www.treasureknit.com/

37.   http://www.visionbedding.com/

38.   http://www.ontapestry.com/

http://www.bagettes.com[40]
http://www.inkchaser.com[41]
http://www.smugmug.com[42]
http://www.michaels.com[43]
http://www.joann.com[44]
http://www.ishopindie.com[45]
http://www.indiecollective.net[46]
http://www.save-on-crafts.com[47]
http://folksy.com[48]
http://craftgawker.com[49]
http://www.artfire.com[50]
http://icraftgifts.com[51]
http://www.handmadespark.com[52]
http://www.handmadecatalog.com[53]
http://www.shophandmade.com[54]

39.   http://www.getetched.com/

40.   http://www.bagettes.com/

41.   http://www.inkchaser.com/poster-printing

42.   http://www.smugmug.com/

43.   http://www.michaels.com/

44.   http://www.joann.com/

45.   http://www.ishopindie.com/

46.   http://www.indiecollective.net/

47.   http://www.save-on-crafts.com/

48.   http://folksy.com/

49.   http://craftgawker.com/

50.   http://www.artfire.com/

51.   http://icraftgifts.com/

52.   http://www.handmadespark.com/

53.   http://www.handmadecatalog.com/

http://indiecraftdocumentary.blogspot.com[55]

http://www.goinghometoroost.com[56]

http://www.craftster.org[57]

http://manmadediy.com[58]

http://www.craftnetwork.com[59]

http://www.hearthandmadeblog.com[60]

http://www.craftbits.com[61]

http://alittlehut.com[62]

http://www.homeofthesampler.com[63]

http://cutique.com/show_dept.php?dept_id=52

http://www.scoutiegirl.com[64]

http://www.acmoore.com/forum/yaf_forum13_crafting-with-robin—fun-project-ideas.aspx[65]

http://www.handmadeology.com[66]

http://ukhandmade.co.uk[67]

54.   http://www.shophandmade.com/

55.   http://indiecraftdocumentary.blogspot.com/

56.   http://www.goinghometoroost.com/

57.   http://www.craftster.org/

58.   http://manmadediy.com/

59.   http://www.craftnetwork.com/

60.   http://www.hearthandmadeblog.com/

61.   http://www.craftbits.com/

62.   http://alittlehut.com/

63.   http://www.homeofthesampler.com/

64.   http://www.scoutiegirl.com/

65.   http://www.acmoore.com/forum/yaf_forum13_crafting-with-robin--fun-project-ideas.aspx

66.   http://www.handmadeology.com/

67.   http://ukhandmade.co.uk/

http://www.buyolympia.com/q

http://www.thehandmademarket.com[68]

http://papernstitch.com[69]

http://www.zibbet.com[70]

http://www.instructables.com[71]

http://www.notmartha.org[72]

http://www.supermarkethq.com[73]

http://www.novica.com[74]

http://www.silkfair.com[75]

http://www.ifnbooks.com[76]

http://www.beaducation.com[77]

http://www.sewingstars.com[78]

---

68.   http://www.thehandmademarket.com/

69.   http://papernstitch.com/

70.   http://www.zibbet.com/

71.   http://www.instructables.com/

72.   http://www.notmartha.org/

73.   http://www.supermarkethq.com/

74.   http://www.novica.com/

75.   http://www.silkfair.com/

76.   http://www.ifnbooks.com/

77.   http://www.beaducation.com/

78.   http://www.sewingstars.com/

Public Domain Resources:

http://www.usa.gov/Citizen/Topics/All-Topics.shtml[1]
    http://www.usa.gov[2]
    http://www.gpo.gov[3]
    http://www.defense.gov[4]
    http://www.archives.org[5]
    http://www.nsa.gov/research/publications/index.shtml
    http://onlinebooks.library.upenn.edu/cce
    http://www.america.gov[6]
    http://www.usa.gov/Topics/Graphics.shtml
    http://beinecke.library/yale.edu/digitallibrary
    http://uwdc.library.wisc.edu/collections/DLDecArts
    http://www.cs.arizona.edu/patterns/weaving
    http://www.biolib.de[7]
    http://answers.usa.gov[8]
    http://www.medline.com/home.jsp
    http://www.howto.gov[9]
    http://librivox.org[10]

---

1. http://www.usa.gov/Citizen/Topics/All-Topics.shtml

2.   http://www.usa.gov/

3.   http://www.gpo.gov/

4.   http://www.defense.gov/

5.   http://www.archives.org/

6.   http://www.america.gov/

7.   http://www.biolib.de/

8.   http://answers.usa.gov/

9.   http://www.howto.gov/

10.   http://librivox.org/

http://nimh.nih.gov/index.shtml
http://www.voanews.com/english/news
http://womenshealth.gov[11]
http://clinicaltrials.gov[12]
http://www.google.com/patents
http://books.google.com[13]
http://www.archive.org[14]
http://www.hathitrust.org[15]
http://www.gutenberg.org[16]

---

11.   http://womenshealth.gov/

12.   http://clinicaltrials.gov/

13.   http://books.google.com/

14.   http://www.archive.org/

15.   http://www.hathitrust.org/

16.   http://www.gutenberg.org/

Music / Audio:

www.librivox.org
   www.musopen.com
   www.pdsounds.org
   www.voanews.com

Public Domain Comics:

http://goldenagecomics.co.uk/index.php[1]
http://www.seegh.com/extchanger
http://www.comicvine.com[2]
Pdsh.wikia.com
http://www.comicbookplus.com[3]
http://www.digitalcomicmuseum.com[4]
http://www.thecomicbooks.com/comics.html
http://www.furycomics/com
http://www.comicstriplibrary.org[5]

---

1. http://goldenagecomics.co.uk/index.php

2.   http://www.comicvine.com/

3.   http://www.comicbookplus.com/

4.   http://www.digitalcomicmuseum.com/

5.   http://www.comicstriplibrary.org/

Niche Research & Competition Research:

http://picniche.com[1]

http://craftcount.com[2]

http://onlinekeywordtool.com[3]

http://trendsresearchtool.com[4]

http://www.patelenterprise.net[5]

http://www.naturalreaders.com/index.htm

http://www.wordstream.com[6]

http://www.findphotokeywords.com[7]

---

1. http://picniche.com/

2.   http://craftcount.com/

3.   http://onlinekeywordtool.com/

4.   http://trendsresearchtool.com/

5.   http://www.patelenterprise.net/

6.   http://www.wordstream.com/

7.   http://www.findphotokeywords.com/

Free & Paid Photos Resources

http://commons.wikimedia.org/wiki/Category:Holidays[1]
  http://www.scriptorium.columbia.edu[2]
http://visipix.com[3]
http://www.loc.gov/library/libarch-digital.html
http://www.loc.gov/search/?q=astronauts&sp=6
http://www.loc.gov/pictures/collection/dag/item/2009632801
http://depositphotos.com[4]
http://office.microsoft.com/en-us/images
http://www.wired.com/rawfile/2011/11/creative-commons
http://www.publicdomainpictures.net[5]
http://public-domain.zorger.com/thumbs/search.php?keyword=woman&search=search
  http://www.photos8.com[6]
http://www.fotosearch.com/photos-images/flea-market.html
http://commons.wikimedia.org/wiki/Main_Page
http://freeimagefiles.com/browse/1
http://www.photogen.com[7]
http://www.vectorportal.com[8]
http://vector4free.com[9]

---

1. http://commons.wikimedia.org/wiki/Category:Holidays

2.   http://www.scriptorium.columbia.edu/

3.   http://visipix.com/

4.   http://depositphotos.com/

5.   http://www.publicdomainpictures.net/

6.   http://www.photos8.com/

7.   http://www.photogen.com/

8.   http://www.vectorportal.com/

http://www.hasslefreeclipart.com[10]

http://www.internetclipart.com[11]

http://www.pdphoto.org[12]

http://vintageprintable.com/wordpress

http://depositphotos.com[13]

http://www.artifactpuzzles.com[14]

http://digitalgallery.nypl.org/nypldigital/explore/dgex-plore.cfm?topic=all&col_id=182

http://www.freedigitalphotos.net[15]

http://www.freephotos.se[16]

http://sxc.hu[17]

http://www.rgbstock.com[18]

http://morguefile.com[19]

http://search.creativecommons.org[20]

http://www.istockphoto.com[21]

http://www.dreamstime.com[22]

9.   http://vector4free.com/

10.   http://www.hasslefreeclipart.com/

11.   http://www.internetclipart.com/

12.   http://www.pdphoto.org/

13.   http://depositphotos.com/

14.   http://www.artifactpuzzles.com/

15.   http://www.freedigitalphotos.net/

16.   http://www.freephotos.se/

17.   http://sxc.hu/

18.   http://www.rgbstock.com/

19.   http://morguefile.com/

20.   http://search.creativecommons.org/

21.   http://www.istockphoto.com/

22.   http://www.dreamstime.com/

http://graphicriver.net[23]
http://www.123rf.com[24]
http://prphotos.net[25]
http://www.fotolia.com[26]
http://www.bigstockphoto.com[27]
http://www.veer.com[28]
http://stockfresh.com[29]
http://www.maxximages.com[30]
http://www.colourlovers.com[31]
http://www.google.com/webfonts
http://www.wordle.net[32]
http://www.freephotos.se[33]
http://www.nasaimages.org[34]
http://aarinfreephoto.com[35]
http://www.freefoto.com/index.jsp
http://www.freeimages.co.uk[36]

23.   http://graphicriver.net/

24.   http://www.123rf.com/

25.   http://prphotos.net/

26.   http://www.fotolia.com/

27.   http://www.bigstockphoto.com/

28.   http://www.veer.com/

29.   http://stockfresh.com/

30.   http://www.maxximages.com/

31.   http://www.colourlovers.com/

32.   http://www.wordle.net/

33.   http://www.freephotos.se/

34.   http://www.nasaimages.org/

35.   http://aarinfreephoto.com/

36.   http://www.freeimages.co.uk/

http://www.freemediagoo.com[37]

http://www.freestockphotos.com[38]

http://office.microsoft.com/en-us/clipart/default.aspx

http://www.inmagine.com[39]

http://www.jupiterimages.com/RoyaltyFreePhotos

http://www.gettyimages.com/creativeimages/royaltyfree

http://www.stockfootageforfree.com[40]

http://www.theclipartsite.com[41]

http://www.clipartgallery.com[42]

http://www.clipart.com/en

http://www.1clipart.com[43]

http://stockvault.net[44]

http://www.princetonol.com/groups/iad/links/clipart.html

---

37.   http://www.freemediagoo.com/

38.   http://www.freestockphotos.com/

39.   http://www.inmagine.com/

40.   http://www.stockfootageforfree.com/

41.   http://www.theclipartsite.com/

42.   http://www.clipartgallery.com/

43.   http://www.1clipart.com/

44.   http://stockvault.net/

Inspirational Photos - Just For Inspiration:

http://knowyourmeme.com[1]
   http://pixabay.com[2]
   http://www.reddit.com/r/aww
   http://moviecitynews.com/2010/1/fill-in-the-caption
   http://www.photofunia.com[3]
   http://funphotobox.com[4]
   http://www.loonapix.com[5]
   http://www.funnywow.com[6]
   http://www.faceinhole.com[7]

---

1. http://knowyourmeme.com/

2.   http://pixabay.com/

3.   http://www.photofunia.com/

4.   http://funphotobox.com/

5.   http://www.loonapix.com/

6.   http://www.funnywow.com/

7.   http://www.faceinhole.com/

Cool Image Tools & Image Editing Tools:

www.tineye.com[1]

    http://fbviralimagecreator.com/one-image

    http://www.shrinkpictures.com[2]

    http://www.littlewebhut.com/gimp

    http://www.gimpshop.com[3]

    http://pixlr.com[4]

    http://www.picmonkey.com[5]

    http://www.aviary.com[6]

    http://www.sumopaint.com[7]

    http://www.colorschemedesigner.com[8]

    http://www.splashup.com[9]

    http://www.resizeyourimage.com[10]

    http://www.webresizer.com[11]

    http://fotoflexer.com[12]

---

1. http://www.tineye.com/

2. http://www.shrinkpictures.com/

3. http://www.gimpshop.com/

4. http://pixlr.com/

5. http://www.picmonkey.com/

6. http://www.aviary.com/

7. http://www.sumopaint.com/

8. http://www.colorschemedesigner.com/

9. http://www.splashup.com/

10. http://www.resizeyourimage.com/

11. http://www.webresizer.com/

12. http://fotoflexer.com/

More Cool Image Editing Tools:

http://www.inkscape.org[1]

http://www.freeserifsoftware.com/software/DrawPlus/default.asp

http://download.microsoft.com/download/a/5/d/a5d625a5-2e3d-4e9c-8608-6de48d7b569f/CreatureHouseExpression3_3.exe[2]

http://www.getpaint.net/index.html

http://gimpshopdotnet.blogspot.com[3]

http://www.freeserifsoftware.com/software/PhotoPlus/default.asp

http://www.freeserifsoftware.com/software/3dPlus/default.asp

http://www.daz3d.com/i.x/software/studio/-/?

http://www.blender.org[4]

http://fotoflexer.com[5]

http://www.getpaint.net[6]

http://download.cnet.com/Serif-PhotoPlus-Starter-Edition/3000-2192_4-75547686.html

http://www.corel.com/corel/product[7]

http://itunes.apple.com/gb/app/id329670577?mt=8

---

1. http://www.inkscape.org/

2. http://download.microsoft.com/download/a/5/d/a5d625a5-2e3d-4e9c-8608-%0D

3. http://gimpshopdotnet.blogspot.com/

4. http://www.blender.org/

5. http://fotoflexer.com/

6. http://www.getpaint.net/

7. http://www.corel.com/corel/product/index.jsp?pid=prod4220093&cid=catalog20038&segid=2500062

http://instagram.com[8]

---

8.   http://instagram.com/

Computer Art And Drawing Programs

http://www.smartdraw.com[1]

http://sketch-master.en.softonic.com[2]

http://www.tuxpaint.org[3]

http://kidspainter.eusoftware.com[4]

http://stuntsoftware.com/freeform

http://www.artamata.com/artists_touch.html

http://itunes.apple.com/us/app/paint-studio-jr/id362954754?mt=8[5]

http://itunes.apple.com/us/app/sketchbook-pro/id364253478?mt=8[6]

http://itunes.apple.com/us/app/quill/id362239305?mt=8

http://itunes.apple.com/us/app/omnigraffle/id363225984?mt=8

http://mudcu.be/sketchpad

http://create.visual.ly[7]

http://www.onemotion.com/flash/sketch-paint

http://www.sumopaint.com/home

http://www.queeky.com/app

http://flockdraw.com[8]

---

1. http://www.smartdraw.com/

2. http://sketch-master.en.softonic.com/

3. http://www.tuxpaint.org/

4. http://kidspainter.eusoftware.com/

5. https://itunes.apple.com/us/app/paint-studio-jr/id362954754?mt=8

6. https://itunes.apple.com/us/app/sketchbook-pro/id364253478?mt=8

7. http://create.visual.ly/

8. http://flockdraw.com/

http://www.dabbleboard.com[9]

---

9. http://www.dabbleboard.com/

The Next Step

In order to learn some additional aspects that you needs to know about sewing, I have included my 70+ Sewing Resources and my 250+ Creative & Inspirational Craft Resources for you. I have also included a section called Interactive Ways For More Cool Sewing Nuggets that will give you some more expert tips and hacks to become more effective with your sewing skills. Just go to these sections of the book to find the specific information.

Once you have gathered enough information on a mental level, the next step is to pick your favorite sewing stitches and techniques and to get into the practical phase of sewing. Pick an easy sewing project that you can accomplish over the weekend and get yourself into the operational phase of sewing.

Like this you will quickly find out if you qualify to become a passionate master of sewing or if you need to look into other crafting options.

If you like to stick with sewing, you will become a master at it if you are practicing your sewing skills and develop a skill for more and more advanced sewing techniques.

In this case, you can go back to the Resources section and the Interactive Ways Of More Cool Sewing Nuggets section in order to continue your sewing path and to learn more advanced techniques. You can also take some advanced sewing technique classes and develop a very lucrative sewing business out of your sewing skills and passions like I talk about it in my From Passion To Profit book series. You can find it in the New Releases section of this book.

If you stick to your sewing passion, you will be able to find many profitable sewing opportunities that you can tap into and develop a lucrative business out of it. The key is to develop a unique product line and stick to a marketing plan that involves Zero Cost Marketing like I talk about in my "From Passion To Profit" book series and in my "Ultimate Crafting Resource Guide Series". Please check out the New Releases section of this book if you'd like to continue with your sewing learning path.

Ah, and one more thing, as a surprise bonus, I have included a fun little quiz for you in order to test your basic knowledge of what you have learned about sewing so far.

If you are able to solve the quiz with no problem, you definitely qualify for continuing your sewing path. In this case, you probably might stick with sewing as your favorite craft.

To get started with the quiz just proceed to the Quiz section and look for 12 basic sewing terms in order to solve the quiz.

Get a sheet of paper and give yourself enough space to write down the 12 sewing terms that you should be looking for.

You can be very creative and look for the terms that are written in all kinds of directions and not only from left to right.

Keep looking from up to down and vice versa.

If you are stuck, keep looking from the perspective of all possible directions that you can think of.

I hope these little hints help you solve the quiz and write down the 12 basic sewing terms on your piece of paper.

Once you are done, you can verify if your answers are correct by looking up the answers in the next chapter that is titled Quiz Results.

You can play this game with a friend or with a group of people and you can make it more exciting by rewarding the winner with a nice treat.

Good luck with the quiz and I wish you a very successful next step where you actually go ahead and go through the
active sewing phase of the process...

One Last Tip For Beginners:

Have a good night of sleep before you get started with your first sewing project in the morning so that you get started with a high energy level.

Bring enough fresh water because this is a very dehydrating process.

Bring fresh fruits and an energy bar to keep up your energy.

I like to prepare a fresh smoothie in the morning before I get started to reward myself with my favorite drink.

Rewarding yourself is a good tactic when you are going through the operational phase because you will see that the experience itself is going to be very tough in the beginning.

Rewarding yourself from time to time with some of your favorite food items that are healthy at the same time is going to be the best way that you can tackle this new experience that is loaded with a new set of emotions that you have to go through at first.

Sewing Quiz

```
G B R O J E E N K V P V X E H
M V P M S E W I N G A Q O M Q
B L N G V S O E P W T J X U F
J T F N W A T P Q X T Q S G T
R Q B I T J D I F L E L T X B
O T R H U F X C T U R P A O F
N R E C M R W X I C N T E S C
K A G T E E X Q M K H D L F T
Y D N I N N L Q E P E E P P X
T B I T D C C N I A V N S L N
F B S S I H X O P A R H K T R
A G M C N S B U T T E R I C K
R G P C G E L D E E N R A M B
C Y T J I A O S K D H O H B A
C Q I A B M V J M U Q Y R U C
```

Correct Quiz Answers

1. Stitching
   2. Singer
   3. French Seam
   4. Dart
   5. Mending
   6. Stitching
   7. Craft
   8. Butterick
   9. Pattern
   10. Stitches
   11. Pleats
   12. Needle

About the Publisher

InfinitYou is a hybrid general interest trade publisher. One of the first of its kind InfinitYou publishes physical books, electronic books, and audiobooks in various genres. Our publications are meant to educate, edify and entertain readers of all walks of life from babies to the elderly. Home to more than twenty imprints such as Infinit Baby, Infinit Kids, Infinit Girl, Infinit Boy, Infinit Coloring, Infinit Swear Words, Infinit Activities, Infinit Productivity, Infinit Cat, Infinit Dog, Infinit Love, Infinit Family, Infinit Survival, Infinit Health, Infinit Beauty, Infinit Spirituality, Infinit Lifestyle, Infinit Wealth, Infinit Romance, and lots more.